TRAINS
on the Move

Willow Clark

PowerKiDS
press™

New York

To Dan, from Penn Station to Copiague and back again

Published in 2010 by The Rosen Publishing Group, Inc.
29 East 21st Street, New York, NY 10010

First Edition

Editor: Nicole Pristash
Book Design: Kate Laczynski
Photo Researcher: Jessica Gerweck

Photo Credits: Cover, pp. 1, 4, 8, 20 Shutterstock.com; p. 6 Andrew Joseph Russell/MPI/Getty Images; p. 10 © Knut Schulz/age fotostock; p. 12 De Agostini Picture Library/Getty Images; pp. 14–15 John William Banagan/Getty Images; p. 16 © VWPICS/age fotostock; p. 18 Koichi Kamoshida/Getty Images.

Library of Congress Cataloging-in-Publication Data

Clark, Willow.
  Trains on the move / Willow Clark. — 1st ed.
      p. cm. — (Transportation station)
  Includes index.
  ISBN 978-1-4358-9331-3 (library binding) — ISBN 978-1-4358-9750-2 (pbk.) — ISBN 978-1-4358-9751-9 (6-pack)
  1. Railroad trains—Juvenile literature. I. Title.
  TF148.C52 2010
  625.1—dc22

                                                      2009021776

Manufactured in the United States of America

CPSIA Compliance Information: Batch #WW10PK: For Further Information contact Rosen Publishing, New York, New York at 1-800-237-9932

Contents

Freight trains, such as the one shown here, are used to carry goods long distances.

All Aboard!

Trains are some of the coolest and most useful vehicles in the world. For years, trains have been moving things from place to place. Freight trains carry large amounts of **cargo**. Passenger trains carry people. High-speed trains are special passenger trains that cover **distances** much faster than other types of trains. These super fast trains are changing the way people travel in Europe and in Asia.

Trains can hold more people and goods than cars and trucks can. Having fewer cars and trucks on the road is good for the **environment**. This makes riding on trains a green way to travel.

The first U.S. transcontinental railroad was finished on May 10, 1869, in Promontory Point, Utah. This picture shows the scene that day.

Laying the Tracks

Trainlike transport dates back to the 1500s, when coal miners used wood tracks to move carts. The advancement of the **steam engine** in the 1700s led to the invention of steam-powered trains. The use of these new trains spread across the world in the 1800s.

In the United States, the country's first **transcontinental railroad** was finished in 1869. It connected the East Coast with the West Coast. This railroad made it faster and easier to move people and goods from one part of the country to another. It led to the building of new cities, and it helped businesses grow.

This is a diesel locomotive on a passenger train. A diesel locomotive is what pulls a train along the track.

How Do Trains Work?

Today's trains are made out of steel, and most of them run on steel tracks. When steel wheels move on steel tracks, little **friction** is made. This allows trains to move easily, and it lowers the amount of **fuel** needed to run the train.

In the past, trains were powered by steam engines that used wood or coal for fuel. Today, most trains run on a mix of **diesel** and electricity. Running on a mix of both allows trains to move without using as much fuel. This is important because using less fuel is good for the environment. Some trains run only on electricity. Electric trains do not use fuel at all.

These men are checking a container sitting on a freight train. The goods that are often in the containers carried on freight trains include food, mail, and farm machinery.

Moving Goods

Freight trains are trains that transport cargo, such as bricks and oil, to places where the cargo will be used. Freight trains use different types of cars to carry cargo. Hoppers are cars that carry grain. Other freight trains have boxlike containers that can be placed on trucks and driven from place to place. Freight trains can carry very heavy loads. Some freight trains carry as much cargo as 75 trucks carry!

A freight train moving at full speed can go 80 miles per hour (129 km/h). These trains are important to business because they move large amounts of goods quickly.

12 *Japan's high-speed train system is called the Shinkansen. Here you can see two Shinkansen bullet trains stopped at a station in Tokyo. Pages 14–15: A bullet train.*

Passenger trains are used to carry people from one place to another. Most passenger trains move between 60 and 100 miles per hour (97–161 km/h). In some places, though, high-speed passenger trains are used. High-speed trains travel more than 125 miles per hour (201 km/h). Most of these trains run on electricity, although some use diesel. High-speed trains often look pointed at their ends, which earned them the nickname "**bullet** trains." The bulletlike shape helps the trains reach high speeds.

Passenger trains are used in many parts of the world. High-speed trains are widely used in Europe and in Asia.

INFORMATION STATION

1. The Baltimore and Ohio Railroad opened in 1830. It ran from Baltimore, Maryland, to the Ohio River in Virginia. It was the first westward-bound railroad in America.

2. When the first U.S. transcontinental railroad was finished, a golden **spike** was used to mark the place where the eastern and western railroads met.

3. Andrew Jackson was the first American president to ride on a train.

4. In 2008, Amtrak, a passenger train service, carried nearly 29 million riders.

5 "Maglev" is short for "**magnetic** levitation." "Levitation" means "lifted into the air."

6 "TGV" is short for *train à grande vitesse*, which means "high-speed train" in French.

7 The largest train station in the world by number of **platforms** is New York City's Grand Central Terminal.

TGV trains, such as the one shown here, connect France with several countries in Europe. The trains that go to Belgium and Germany are some of the most heavily traveled TGV trains.

France's Fast Trains

The high-speed train system in France is called TGV. This electric rail system was begun in the early 1970s. Paris is the center of the system. The system then spreads across France and into neighboring countries.

TGV trains are very fast. In 2007, a TGV train set a speed record for a conventional train, which is a train that runs on wheels and a track. This train traveled 357 miles per hour (575 km/h), beating a 1990 record of 320 miles per hour (515 km/h). When carrying passengers, a TGV train's top speed is 199 miles per hour (320 km/h).

18 *Shown here is the maglev train that set the speed record for a nonconventional train on December 2, 2003. The record run took place on a track in Yamanashi, Japan.*

Trains Without Wheels

Maglev, or magnetic levitation, trains are high-speed trains that move using **electromagnets**. The magnetic field created by these electromagnets allows a maglev train to move along the track without touching it. It is like the train is floating! Maglev trains move very quickly. The world speed record for a nonconventional train, one that does not run on wheels and a track, was set in 2003. A Japanese maglev train reached 361 miles per hour (581 km/h)!

Today, China and Japan have passenger maglev train systems. There are also plans to build more systems around the world.

Heavy traffic, such as this, is common on Los Angeles highways. Many people believe that a high-speed rail system in California would help cut down on this problem.

More Trains, Less Traffic

Unlike Asia and Europe, the United States does not have a high-speed rail system. This may change over the next few years, though. In 2009, President Barack Obama talked about plans to build electric high-speed rail systems across the country. Many people believe that building these systems will lighten traffic on roads and help protect the environment.

California may build a high-speed rail system that will connect its biggest cities. A train from Sacramento to San Diego would travel at about 164 miles per hour (264 km/h), covering the 588-mile (946 km) trip in just over 3.5 hours!

Trains in Our World

Trains are an important part of our world. In the past, trains helped countries grow. Today, freight trains move goods quickly and at a lower cost than other shipping methods. Many people travel on passenger trains, which uses less fuel than traveling by car.

Across the world, high-speed trains are allowing people to travel distances faster than they can in cars and in conventional trains. These super fast vehicles are changing the way we travel and are helping keep the world a little greener. The next time you see a train, think about all the ways they help make our world better!

Glossary

bullet (BU-let) Something that is shot out of a gun.

cargo (KAHR-goh) The load of goods carried by a train, an airplane, a ship, or an automobile.

diesel (DEE-zel) A fuel used in engines.

distances (DIS-ten-sez) The lengths between points.

electromagnets (ih-lek-troh-MAG-nets) Magnets made by electricity.

environment (en-VY-ern-ment) All the living things and conditions of a place.

friction (FRIK-shin) The rubbing of one thing against another.

fuel (FYOOL) Something burned to make warmth or power.

magnetic (mag-NEH-tik) Having to do with the force that pulls certain objects toward one another.

platforms (PLAT-fawrmz) Flat, raised areas where people can stand.

spike (SPYK) A sharp, pointy thing shaped like a spear or a needle.

steam engine (STEEM EN-jun) An engine powered by steam.

transcontinental railroad (trants-kon-tuh-NEN-tul RAYL-rohd) The train system that crossed the United States in the 1800s.

Index

Web Sites

Due to the changing nature of Internet links, PowerKids Press has developed an online list of Web sites related to the subject of this book. This site is updated regularly. Please use this link to access the list: www.powerkidslinks.com/stat/train/